Calling all budding springtime spellers!

If you're looking for springtime spelling practice, this brilliant Daily Practice book from CGP will help pupils' spelling skills blossom beautifully!

Inside, you'll find a page of spelling practice for every school day of the spring term, covering vital skills from the Year 1 curriculum.

Easy-to-follow examples mean it's perfect for practice wherever you are — at home, at school or frolicking with the lambs!

What CGP is all about

Our sole aim here at CGP is to produce the highest quality books — carefully written, immaculately presented and dangerously close to being funny.

Then we work our socks off to get them out to you — at the cheapest possible prices.

Contents

☑ Use the tick boxes to help keep a record of which tests have been attempted.

Week 1
- ☑ Day 1 1
- ☑ Day 2 2
- ☑ Day 3 3
- ☑ Day 4 4
- ☑ Day 5 5

Week 2
- ☑ Day 1 6
- ☑ Day 2 7
- ☑ Day 3 8
- ☑ Day 4 9
- ☑ Day 5 10

Week 3
- ☑ Day 1 11
- ☑ Day 2 12
- ☑ Day 3 13
- ☑ Day 4 14
- ☑ Day 5 15

Week 4
- ☑ Day 1 16
- ☑ Day 2 17
- ☑ Day 3 18
- ☑ Day 4 19
- ☑ Day 5 20

Week 5
- ☑ Day 1 21
- ☑ Day 2 22
- ☑ Day 3 23
- ☑ Day 4 24
- ☑ Day 5 25

Week 6
- ☑ Day 1 26
- ☑ Day 2 27
- ☑ Day 3 28
- ☑ Day 4 29
- ☑ Day 5 30

Week 7
- ☑ Day 1 31
- ☑ Day 2 32
- ☑ Day 3 33
- ☑ Day 4 34
- ☑ Day 5 35

Week 8
- ☑ Day 1 36
- ☑ Day 2 37
- ☑ Day 3 38
- ☑ Day 4 39
- ☑ Day 5 40

Week 9
- ☑ Day 1 41
- ☑ Day 2 42
- ☑ Day 3 43
- ☑ Day 4 44
- ☑ Day 5 45

Week 10
- ☑ Day 1 46
- ☑ Day 2 47
- ☑ Day 3 48
- ☑ Day 4 49
- ☑ Day 5 50

Week 11
- ☑ Day 1 51
- ☑ Day 2 52
- ☑ Day 3 53
- ☑ Day 4 54
- ☑ Day 5 55

Week 12
- ☑ Day 1 56
- ☑ Day 2 57
- ☑ Day 3 58
- ☑ Day 4 59
- ☑ Day 5 60

Answers 61

Published by CGP

ISBN: 978 1 78908 832 8

Editors: Keith Blackhall, Tom Carney, Rachel Craig-McFeely, Gabrielle Richardson
With thanks to Andy Cashmore and Juliette Green for the proofreading.
With thanks to Lottie Edwards for the copyright research.

Cover and Graphics used throughout the book © www.edu-clips.com

Printed by Sterling, Kettering.
Based on the classic CGP style created by Richard Parsons.

Text, design, layout and original illustrations© Coordination Group Publications Ltd. (CGP) 2021
All rights reserved.

Photocopying this book is not permitted, even if you have a CLA licence.
Extra copies are available from CGP with next day delivery • 0800 1712 712 • www.cgpbooks.co.uk

How to Use this Book

- This book contains 60 pages of daily spelling practice.

- We've split them into 12 sections — that's roughly one for each week of the Year 1 Spring term.

- Each week is made up of 5 pages, so there's one for every school day of the term (Monday — Friday).

- Each page should take about 10 minutes to complete.

- The words tested are suitable for the Year 1 English curriculum. New words and sounds are gradually introduced through the book.

- The pages increase in difficulty as you progress through the book.

- Answers can be found at the back of the book.

- Each page looks something like this:

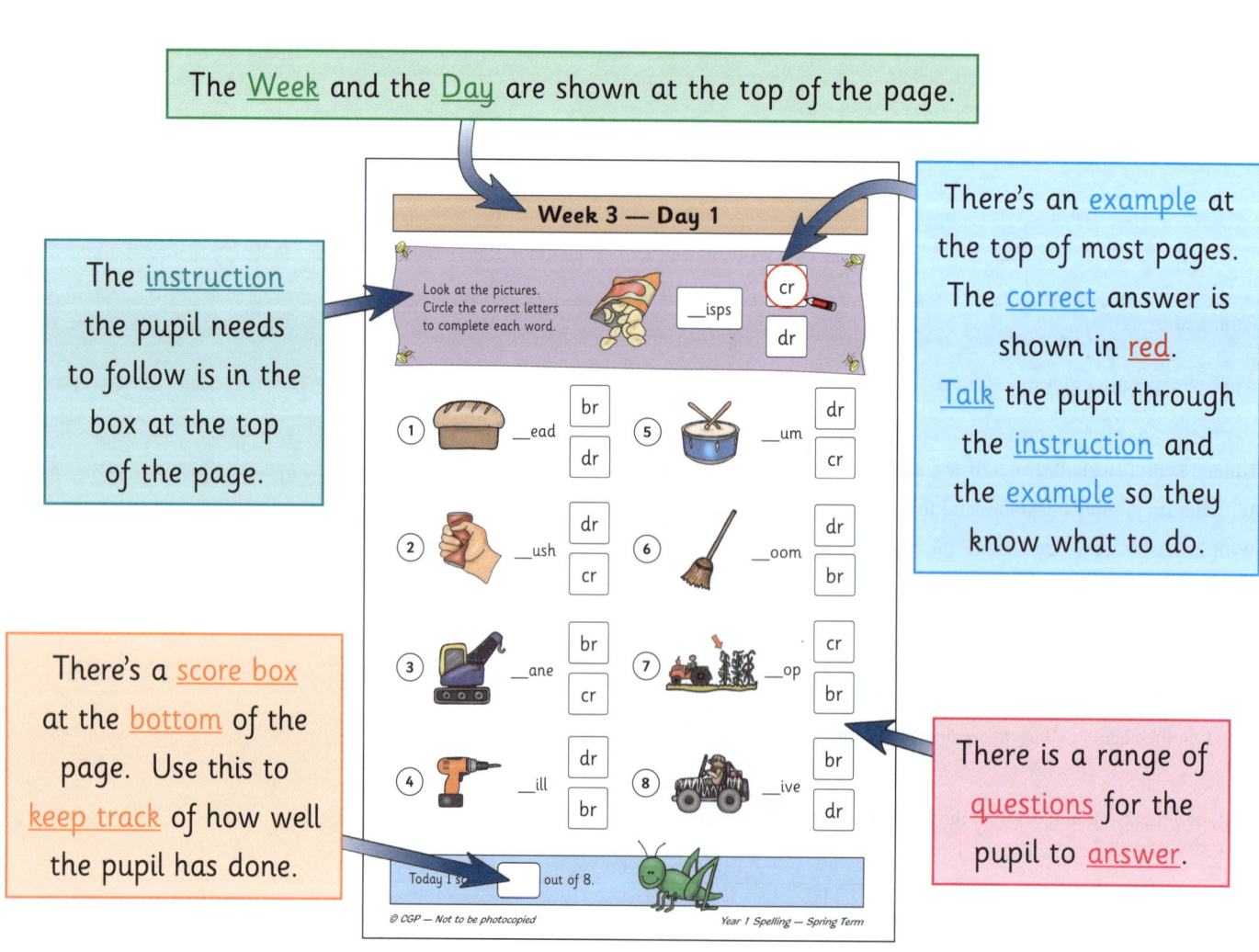

The Week and the Day are shown at the top of the page.

The instruction the pupil needs to follow is in the box at the top of the page.

There's an example at the top of most pages. The correct answer is shown in red. Talk the pupil through the instruction and the example so they know what to do.

There's a score box at the bottom of the page. Use this to keep track of how well the pupil has done.

There is a range of questions for the pupil to answer.

Week 1 — Day 1

Read each pair of words. Colour the picture next to the word that has two syllables.

 bee flower

1.  gate padlock

2.  digging bone

3.  snowy hot

4. 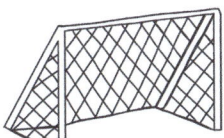 goalpost ball

5.  grapes apple

6.  rabbit mouse

Today I scored ☐ out of 6.

Week 1 — Day 2

Read each sentence. Circle the correct spelling of the word in bold.

Ime rang the **bell** / **bel** .

① A crab lives in that **shell** / **shel** .

 ② Watch out for the **bul** / **bull** !

③ Jim saw me **spil** / **spill** a drink.

 ④ Freja was feeling **ill** / **il** .

⑤ Please do not **yell** / **yel** .

 ⑥ The man sat in a **cel** / **cell** .

⑦ He nearly **fell** / **fel** over.

Today I scored ☐ out of 7.

Week 1 — Day 3

Draw a line to match each picture with the correct spelling.

hatch

hach

1. matsh / match

2. watch / wach

3. pich / pitch

4. hutch / huch

5. scratch / scratsh

6. skech / sketch

Today I scored  out of 6.

Week 1 — Day 4

Look at the pictures. Circle the correct letters to complete each word.

1. __um pl bl

2. __ow pl bl

3. __ate pl bl

4. __ink pl bl

5. __ender pl bl

6. __anet pl bl

Today I scored ☐ out of 6.

Week 1 — Day 5

Read the sentences. Look at the words in bold. Underline all the words that are **not** spelt correctly.

She took **herr** swords.

1) Colin **wos** ready to win **some** prizes.

2) **He** had trained **al** week.

3) Lots of people **wer there** to watch.

4) "Do **you hav** your spear?" the king asked.

5) "**Yess**, I am ready!" **said** Colin.

6) **Me** and **mi** friends saw Colin hit the target.

7) **We** cheered and roared **lyke** dragons.

Today I scored ☐ out of 7.

Week 2 — Day 1

Colour the picture next to the word that is spelt correctly.

| best |  | besst |  |

1. sent  sennt

2. list  listt

3. postt  post

4. vesst  vest

5. bent  bentt

6. bernt  burnt

Today I scored ☐ out of 6.

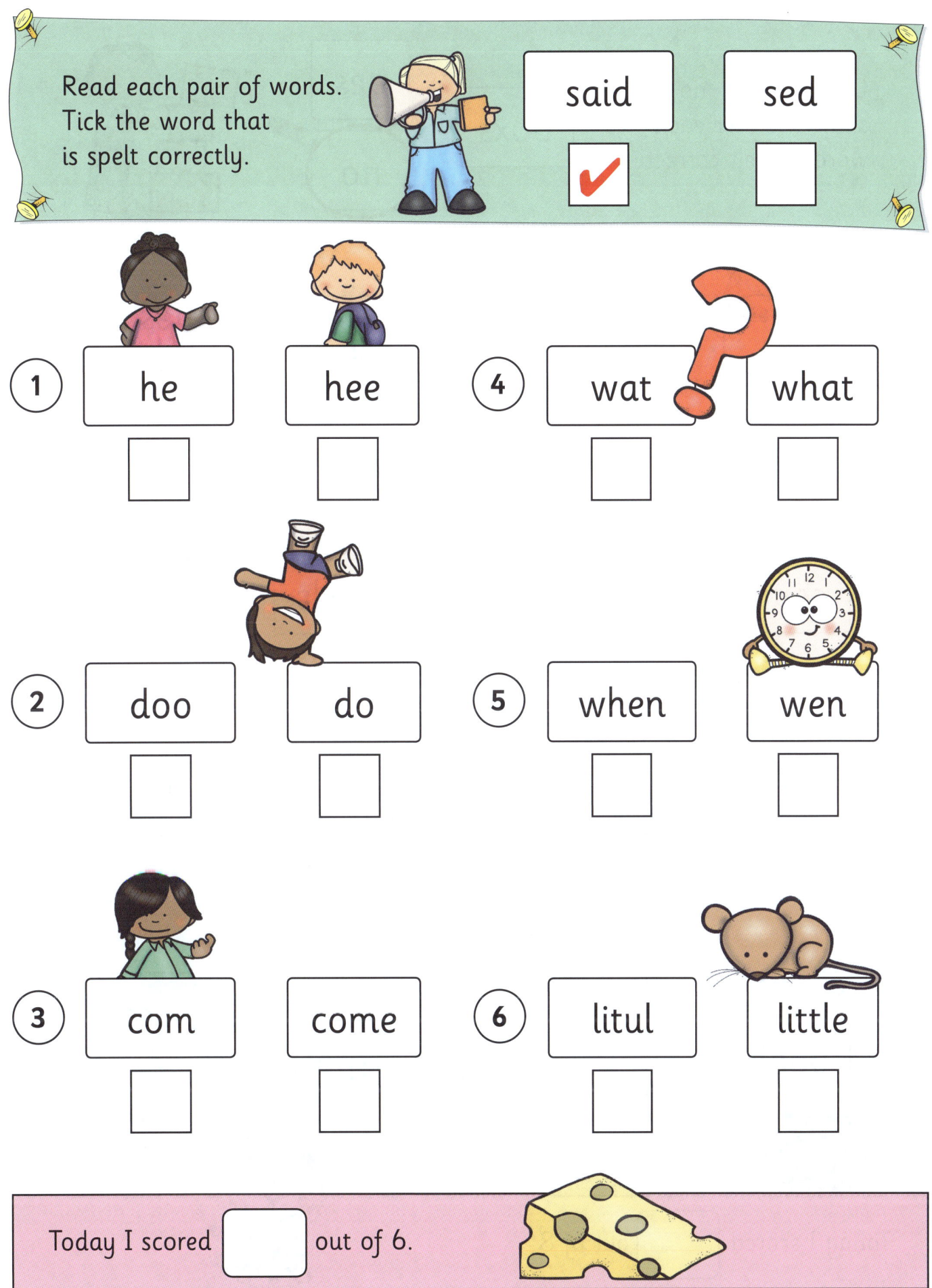

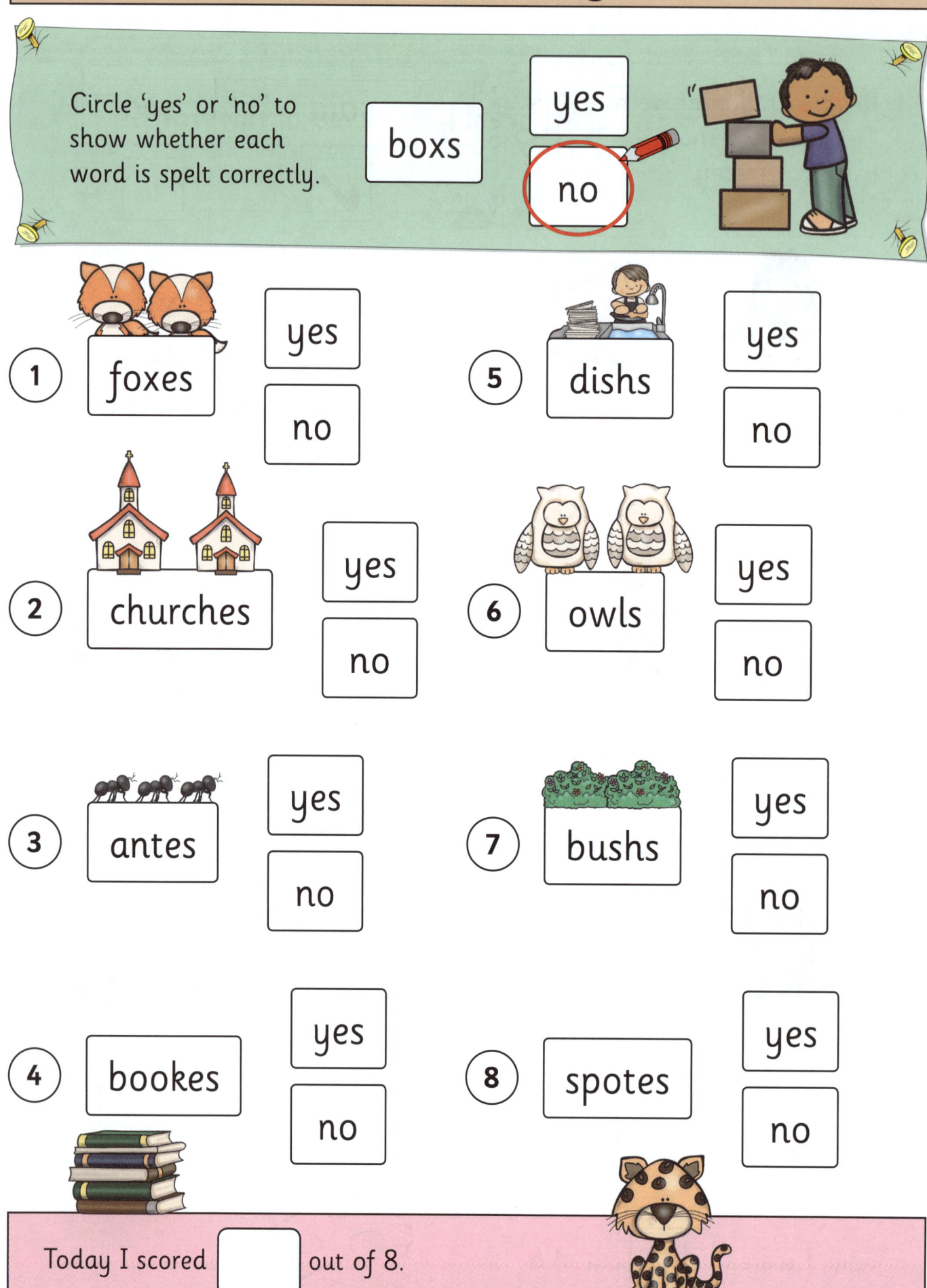

Week 2 — Day 4

Read each pair of sentences. Tick the sentence where the word in bold is spelt correctly.

I was scared of the **wolff**. ☐
I was scared of the **wolf**. ✓

1. The **ellf** danced happily. ☐
   The **elf** danced happily. ☐

2. The wizard lost his **belt**. ☐
   The wizard lost his **bellt**. ☐

3. The witch put the frog on a **shelff**. ☐
   The witch put the frog on a **shelf**. ☐

4. I am wearing a **killt**. ☐
   I am wearing a **kilt**. ☐

5. Jack climbed the **tall** vine. ☐
   Jack climbed the **tal** vine. ☐

6. She went to **sulke**. ☐
   She went to **sulk**. ☐

Today I scored ☐ out of 6.

Week 2 — Day 5

Draw lines to match the words to the correct missing letters. Each word should match the picture shown.

1.  __lat

2.  __eep

3.  __ile

4.  __ooth

sn

sp

sl

sw

sm

5. __ime

6.  __eat

7. 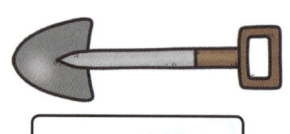 __ade

8.  __ooze

Today I scored ☐ out of 8.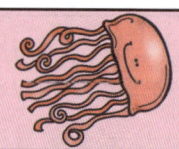

Week 3 — Day 1

Look at the pictures. Circle the correct letters to complete each word.

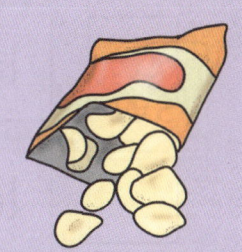 __isps    (cr) / dr

1.  __ead   br / dr

2.  __ush   dr / cr

3.  __ane   br / cr

4.  __ill   dr / br

5.  __um   dr / cr

6.  __oom   dr / br

7.  __op   cr / br

8.  __ive   br / dr

Today I scored [ ] out of 8.

Week 3 — Day 2

Read each pair of words. Tick the word that is spelt correctly.

✓ longest
☐ longgest

1.
☐ highest
☐ highhest

2.
☐ coldest
☐ colddest

3.
☐ shorttest
☐ shortest

4.
☐ quicest
☐ quickest

5.
☐ strongest
☐ stronggest

6.
☐ slowwest
☐ slowest

Today I scored ☐ out of 6.

Week 3 — Day 3

Read each sentence. Colour the picture if the word in bold is spelt correctly.

Mona will **push** the trolley.

(1) **Her** is the beach.

(2) We should **put** suncream on.

(3) Dad **says** we can get ice cream.

(4) The boat will **pul** us on the sea.

(5) The hut **by** the beach.

(6) He **haz** thrown the ball.

Today I scored ☐ out of 6.

Week 3 — Day 4

Read each sentence. Circle the correct spelling of the missing word.

The clock is _____ .   (ticking)   tickking

1. Yaro enjoys _____ up mountains.   gowing   going

2. Shannon is _____ on the sofa.   resting   restting

3. The plane is _____ on the runway.   landing   landding

4. Annie is _____ a question.   askking   asking

5. I like _____ films at the cinema.   watching   watchhing

6. The horse is _____ over the fence.   leapping   leaping

Today I scored ☐ out of 6.

Week 3 — Day 5

Read each sentence. Fill in the gap with '**tr**', '**fr**' or '**gr**' to complete the word.

Mia and Jack are on a ..tr..ek in the forest.

1) Mia sees something huge and ....een.

2) "Oh no, it's a ....oll!" she cries.

3) Jack shakes and ....oans quietly.

4) "It's okay, I'm ....iendly," says the troll.

5) Behind Mia, Jack is ....ozen in fear.

6) "What if it's a ....ick?" he asks.

7) Mia ....ins and goes to say hello.

Today I scored ☐ out of 7.

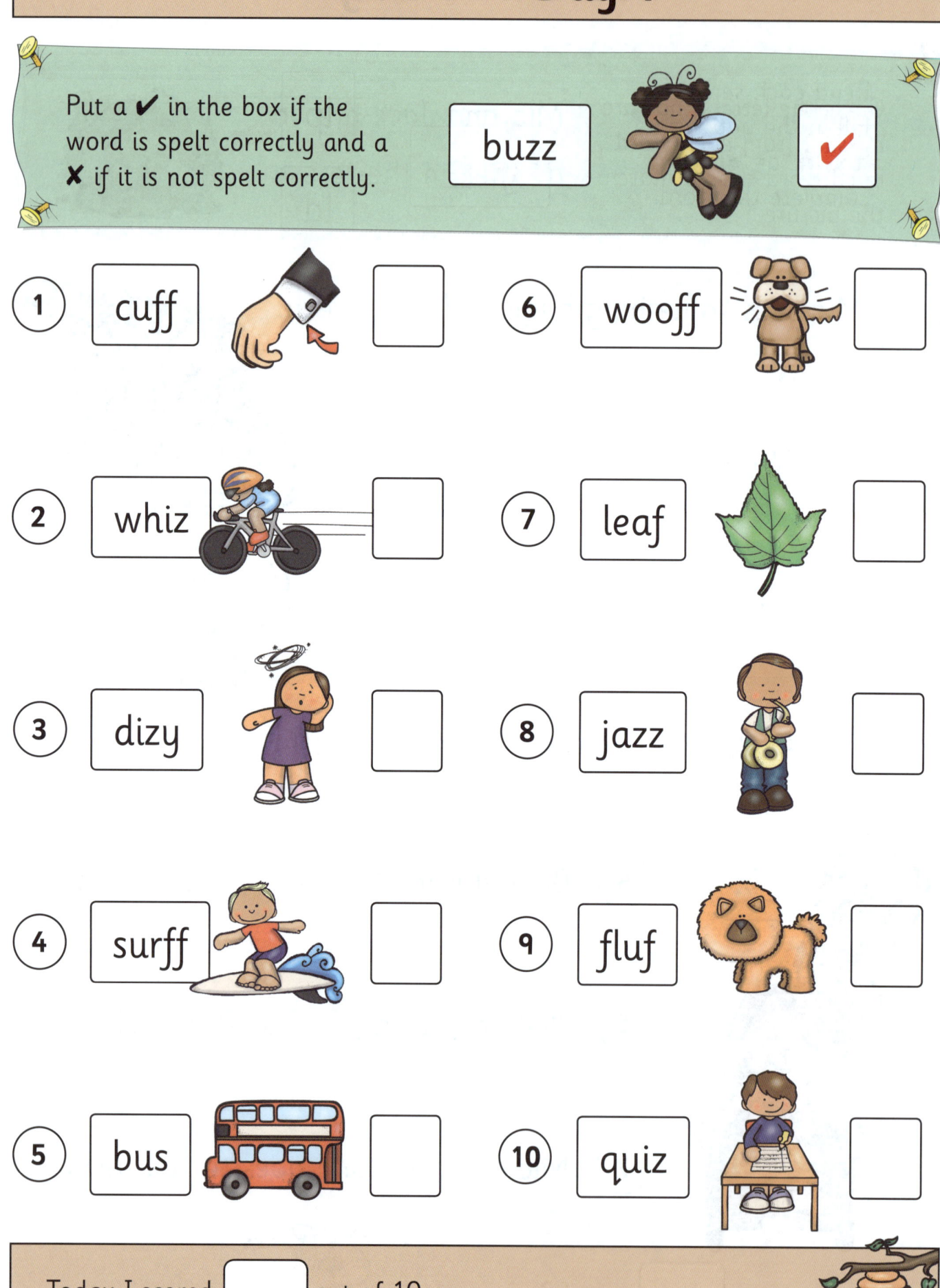

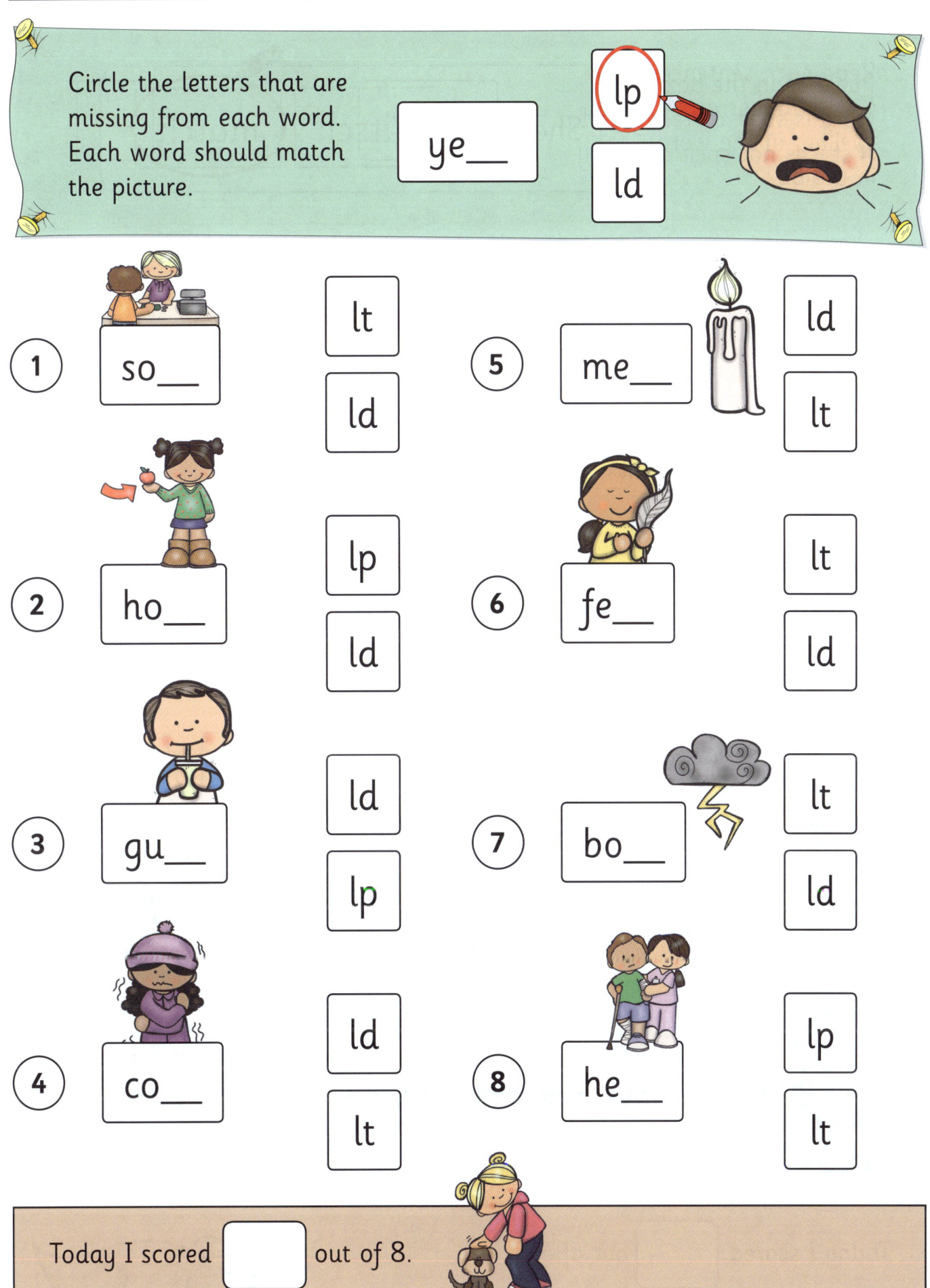

Week 4 — Day 3

Read each sentence. Circle the correct spelling of the word in the box.

She lit a | matsch | (match) .

1. My jumper is | itchy | ichy | .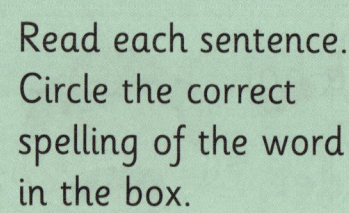

2. My | teatcher | teacher | is friendly.

3. Arham left his shoes in the | porch | portch | .

4. Dad made a | batch | bach | of cookies.

5. We go to the zoo on a | coatch | coach | .

6. I have a pair of | cruches | crutches | .

Today I scored [ ] out of 6.

Week 4 — Day 4

Read each sentence. Circle the word in bold if it is spelt correctly. Underline it if it is **not** spelt correctly.

The (lazy) dog wore a hat.

I help keep things <u>tidee</u>.

(1) Everyone is at Jane's **party**.

(2) We watch the **funnee** clown.

(3) The cake was not **easy** to make.

(4) It is a nice, **sunny** day.

(5) Jane's **familee** are here.

(6) She is **very** glad they came.

(7) Jane is **happi** with her presents.

Today I scored ☐ out of 7.

Week 4 — Day 5

Read the sentence. Circle the letters needed to complete the words.

① Alex heard the goose ho__ .

nk | nck

② The pi__ flamingo had a bath.

nc | nk

③ John's boat has sun_ .

ck | k

④ Ella picked an apple with her tru__ .

nk | nc

⑤ Sarah ran away from the skun_ .

k | ck

⑥ Amy had a dri__ .

nk | nck

Today I scored ☐ out of 6.

Week 5 — Day 1

Read each pair of words. Tick the word that is spelt correctly.

✓ fuller
☐ fuler

1. ☐ soffter
   ☐ softer

2. ☐ quickker
   ☐ quicker

3. ☐ slower
   ☐ slowwer

4. ☐ warmmer
   ☐ warmer

5. ☐ louder
   ☐ loudder

6. ☐ lighter
   ☐ lightr

Today I scored ☐ out of 6.

Week 5 — Day 2

Colour the picture next to the word that is spelt correctly.

1. soc 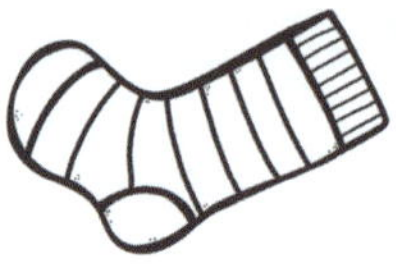 / sock 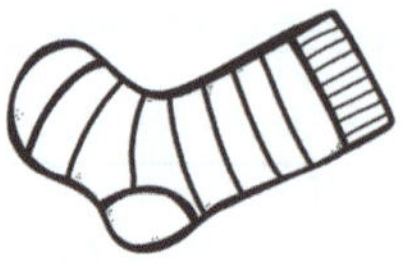
2. kicc 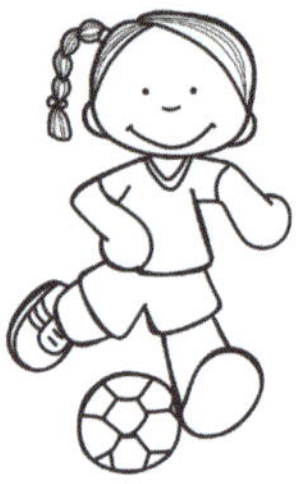 / kick 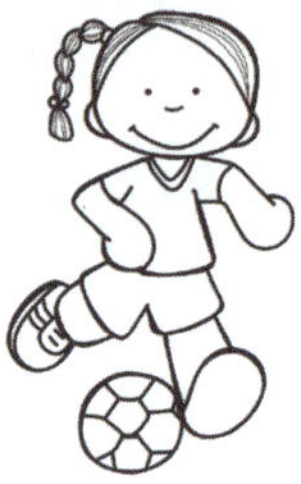
3. back 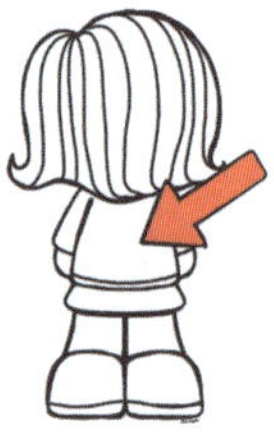 / bak 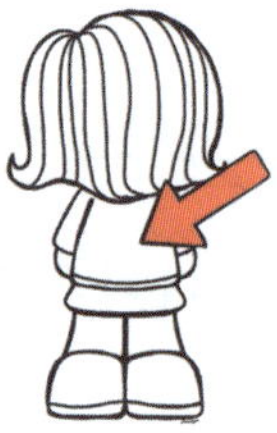
4. park 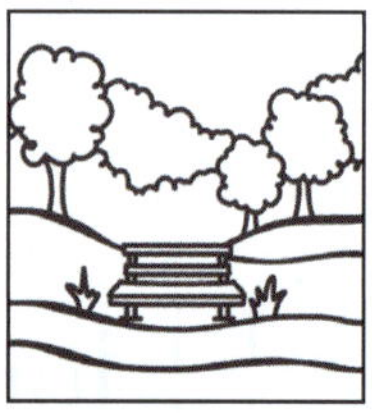 / parck 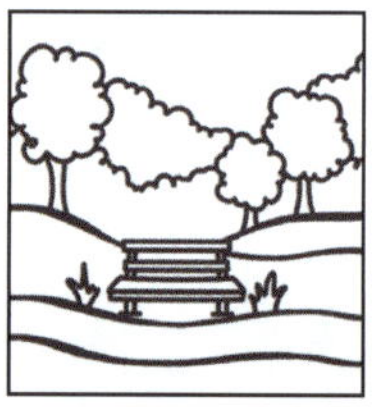
5. lick 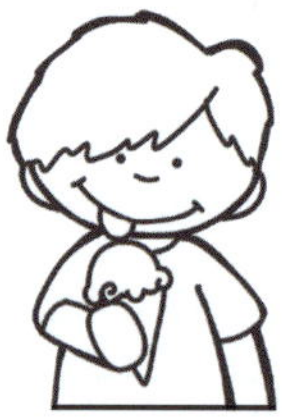 / licc 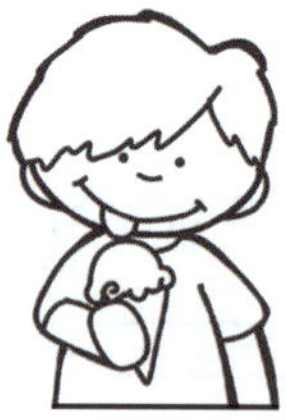
6. shrunck 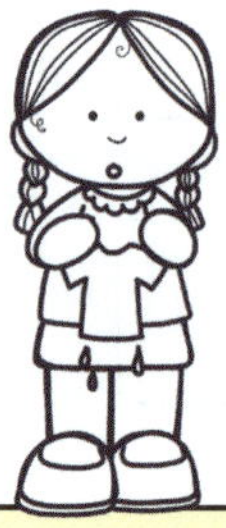 / shrunk

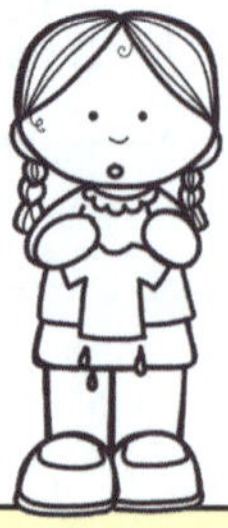

Today I scored ☐ out of 6.

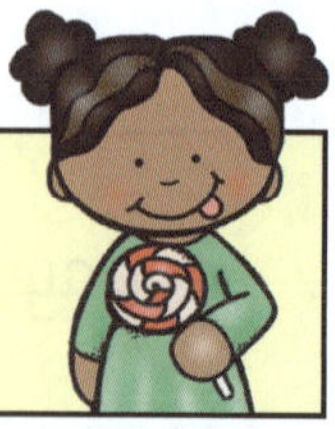

Week 5 — Day 3

Read each sentence. Circle the correct spelling of the word in bold.

I buy **plums** / **pllums** .

1) Be careful not to **sllip** / **slip** !

2) She has a **black** / **blacck** cat.

3) Miles has **bllond** / **blond** hair.

4) The pig **pllods** / **plods** in the mud.

5) My pencil is **bllunt** / **blunt** .

6) He raced down the **slope** / **sloppe** .

Today I scored ☐ out of 6.

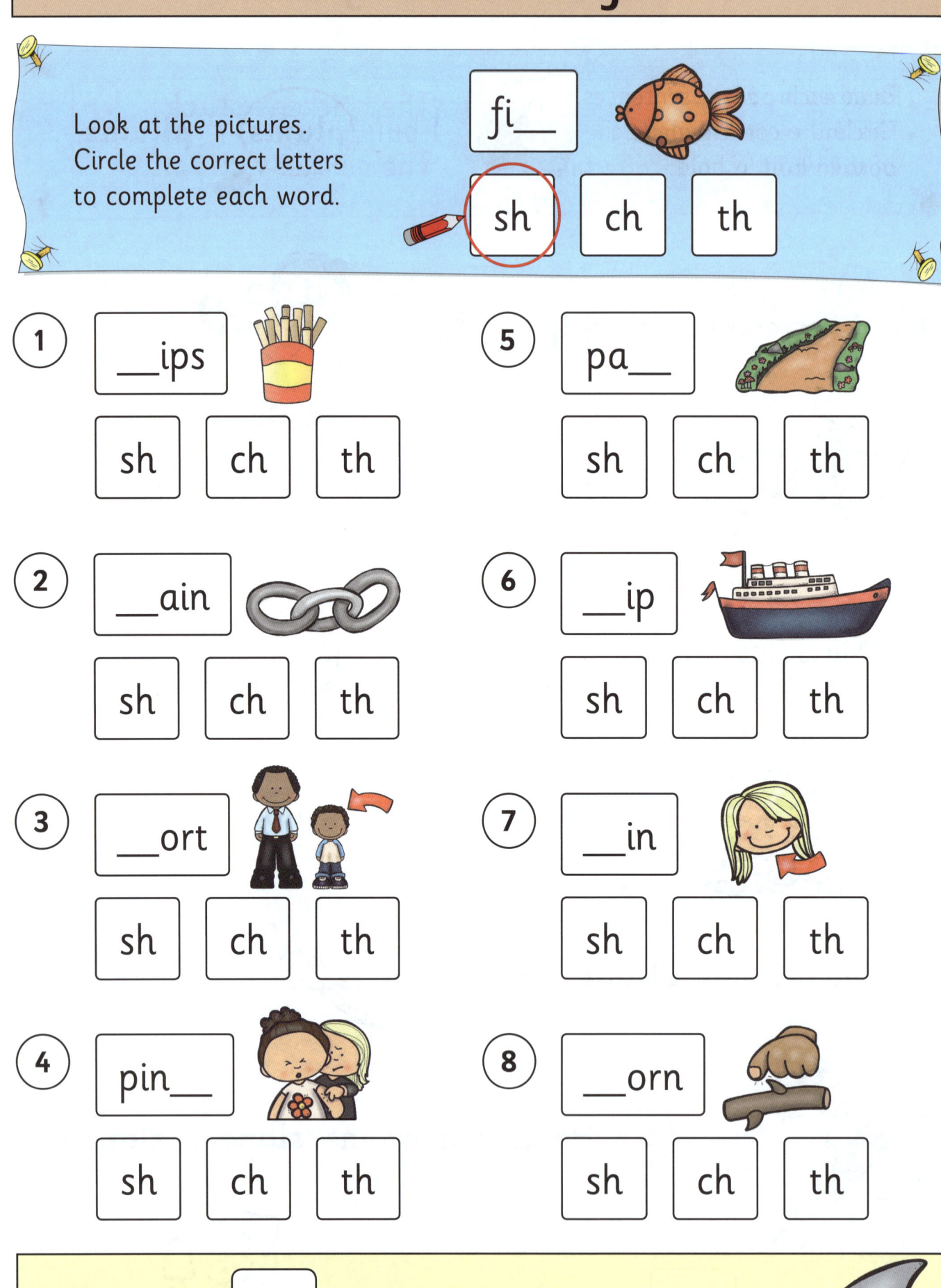

Week 5 — Day 5

Read each pair of sentences. Tick the sentence where the word in bold is spelt correctly.

The chickens **cluck**. ✓
The chickens **clluck**. ☐

1) Yulia is **gladd** she won. ☐
   Yulia is **glad** she won. ☐

2) The moon **glows** in the sky. ☐
   The moon **gllows** in the sky. ☐

3) We make **cllay** pots. ☐
   We make **clay** pots. ☐

4) The **clocck** ticks loudly. ☐
   The **clock** ticks loudly. ☐

5) I can **cllick** my fingers. ☐
   I can **click** my fingers. ☐

6) Jimmy looks at the **globe**. ☐
   Jimmy looks at the **gllobe**. ☐

Today I scored ☐ out of 6.

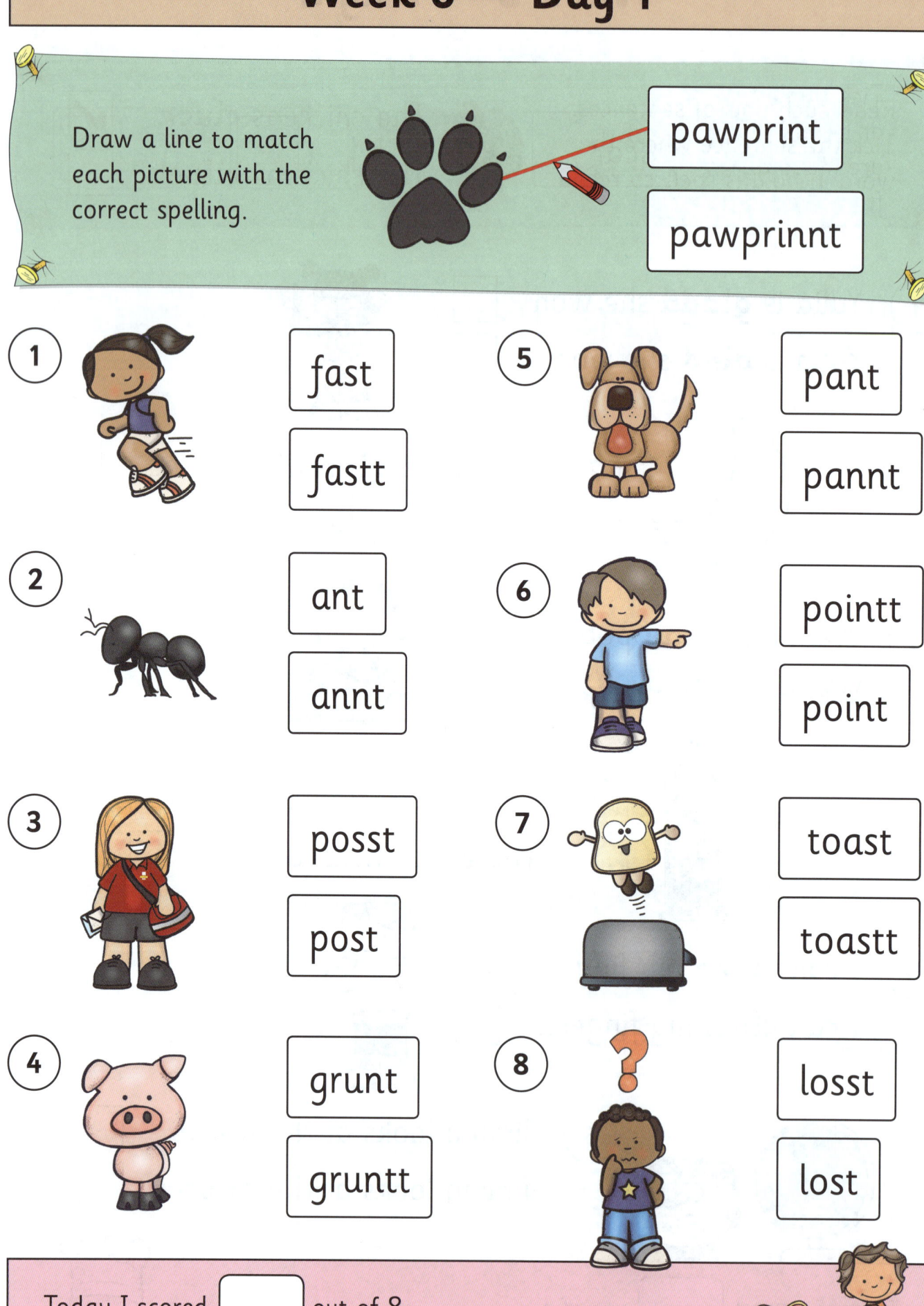

Week 6 — Day 2

Tick the letter or letters that are missing from the word.

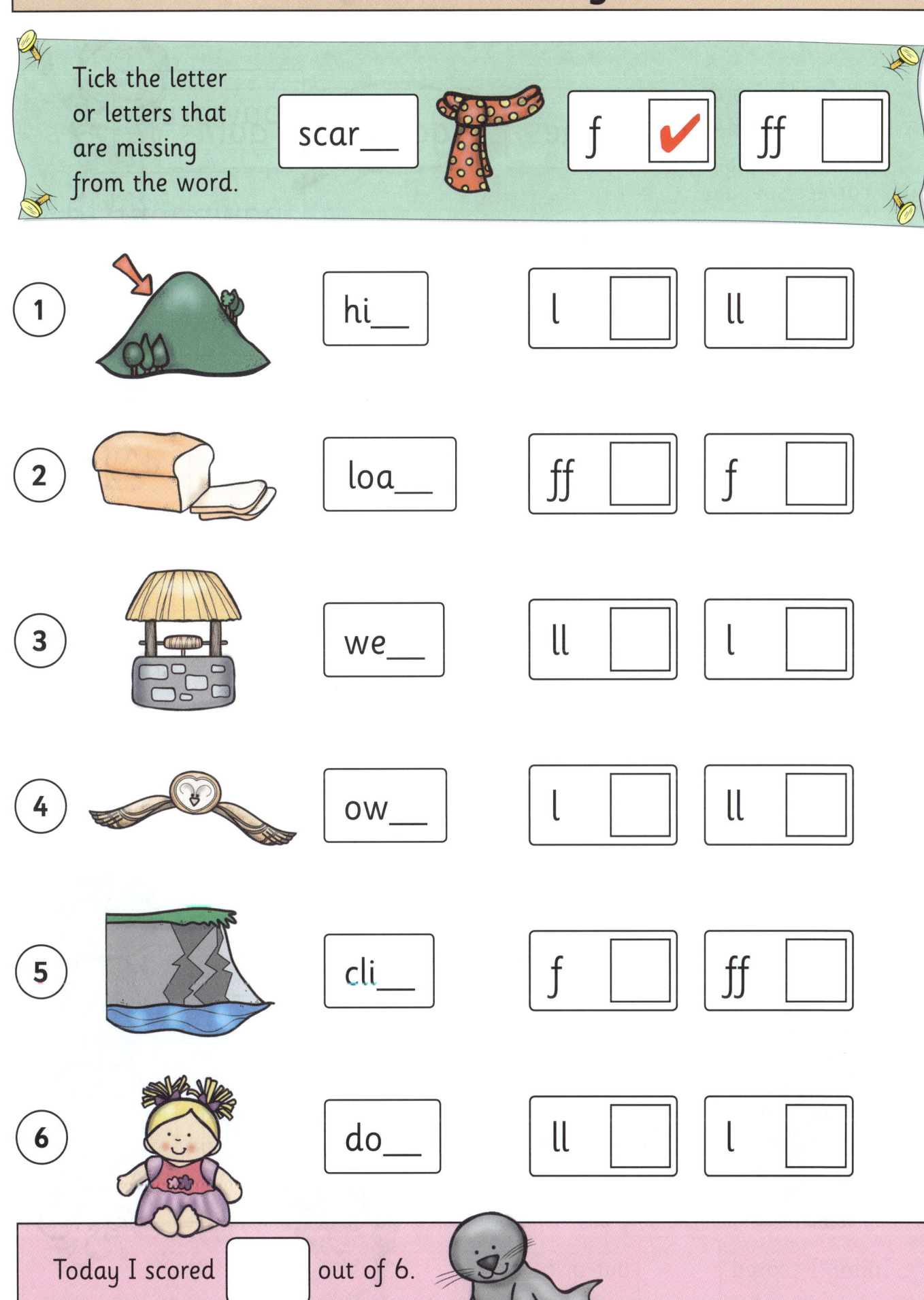

Week 6 — Day 3

Circle the word that has been spelt correctly.

gammes | **(games)** | gams

1. splashes | splashs | splashis
2. sprayys | sprayes | sprays
3. runnes | runs | runns
4. catchs | catchhes | catches
5. drips | dripps | drippes
6. smils | smiles | smilles

Today I scored ☐ out of 6.

Week 6 — Day 4

Read each pair of sentences. Tick the sentence where the word in bold is spelt correctly.

The witches **are** having a party. ✔

The witches **ar** having a party. ☐

1) The party **iz** today. ☐
   The party **is** today. ☐

2) There will **bee** cake. ☐
   There will **be** cake. ☐

3) Bring **yor** wand. ☐
   Bring **your** wand. ☐

4) **No** dragons can come. ☐
   Noo dragons can come. ☐

5) Can you come **too** the party? ☐
   Can you come **to** the party? ☐

Today I scored ☐ out of 5.

Week 6 — Day 5

Read each sentence. Circle 'yes' or 'no' to show whether the word in bold is spelt correctly.

I **spy** with my little eye...

1) A **swwan** with a long neck.   yes   no

2) A very **slimy** slug.   yes   no

3) A green **snake** with stripes.   yes   no

4) A monkey that **sswings** in the trees.   yes   no

5) An insect with black **spotts**.   yes   no

6) A cat that **smells** bad.   yes   no

Today I scored ☐ out of 6.

Week 7 — Day 1

Read each pair of words. Tick the word that is spelt correctly.

honked ✓ honkeed ☐

1. reading ☐
   readding ☐

2. brushedd ☐
   brushed ☐

3. boxr ☐
   boxer ☐

4. eatingg ☐
   eating ☐

5. singer ☐
   singger ☐

6. cheering ☐
   cheerng ☐

7. splashd ☐
   splashed ☐

8. baker ☐
   bakerr ☐

Today I scored ☐ out of 8.

Week 7 — Day 2

Read each sentence. Circle 'yes' or 'no' to show whether the word in bold is spelt correctly.

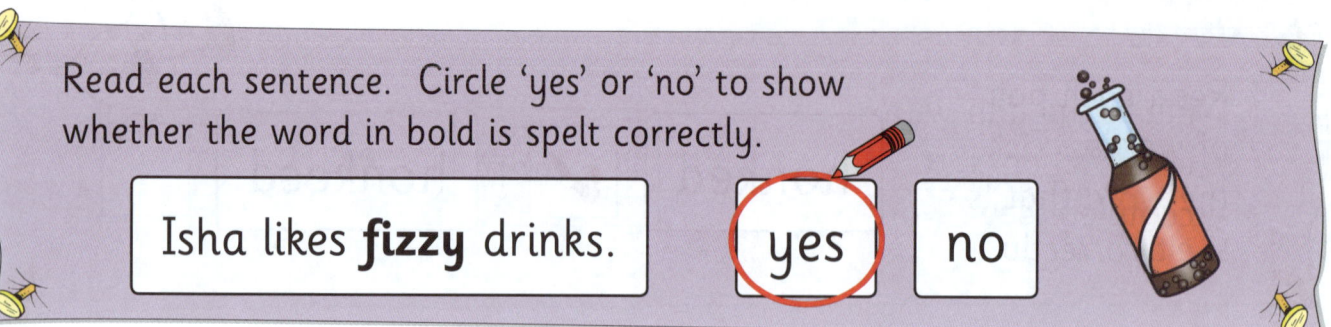

Isha likes **fizzy** drinks.   yes   no

1) Please **pass** me my helmet.   yes   no

2) I hear the **buz** of bees.   yes   no

3) Do not make Rita **cross**.   yes   no

4) Look at the sausages **sizzle**!   yes   no

5) Her **bos** is called Mike.   yes   no

6) I have two **sissters**.   yes   no

Today I scored ☐ out of 6.

Week 7 — Day 3

Fill in the gap with either 'c' or 's' to complete each word.

..s..leep

1) …..law

5) …..lide

2) …..lug

6) …..lub

3) …..limb

7) …..lip

4) …..low

8) …..logs

Today I scored ▢ out of 8.

Week 7 — Day 4

Draw lines between the letters in each box to spell a word. The first letter of the word is red. Use the picture to help you.

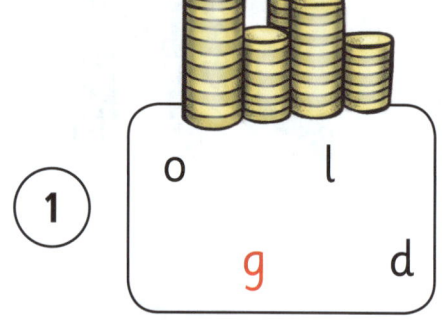

1. o l
   g d

4. **s** l
   a t

2. **c** a
   l f

5. **y** p
   e l

3. **m** k
   i l

6. **a** u t
   d l

Today I scored ☐ out of 6.

Year 1 Spelling — Spring Term

Week 7 — Day 5

Look at the picture and read the sentences. Circle the correct spelling of the words in bold.

That is (unfair) / unffair .

1. Rob feels **unsafe** / **unnsafe** .

2. Jack and Tina **unlload** / **unload** the car.

3. Kim **unnties** / **unties** Atalia's shoelace.

4. Grace **unlocks** / **unnlocks** the door.

5. Imani is **unnhappy** / **unhappy** .

6. Barney is **unwwell** / **unwell** .

Today I scored ☐ out of 6.

Week 8 — Day 2

Colour the picture next to the word that is spelt correctly.

1. frend    friend

2. school    skool

3. luv    love

4. ful    full

5. push    poosh

6. pul    pull

Today I scored [ ] out of 6.

Week 8 — Day 3

Read each sentence, then circle the correct spelling of the word in bold.

Eli rides a **pony** / **poni**.

(1) Adam lifts the **heavy** / **heavvy** weight.

(2) Helen is trying **archeree** / **archery**.

(3) We **enjoey** / **enjoy** rowing.

(4) I was **angry** / **angri** when I lost.

(5) Fred is running the **relay** / **relayy** race.

(6) The winner's medal is really **shinne** / **shiny**.

(7) We **play** / **plai** hockey every day.

Today I scored ☐ out of 7.

Week 8 — Day 4

Read each sentence. Fill in the gap with either '**nt**' or '**st**' to complete the word.

Joe and Cheng were lo…**st**… .

1. They had been walking in the fore………. for hours.

2. "I wa………. to go home!" said Joe.

3. "Let's sit down and re……….," sighed Cheng.

4. They sat down by a big pla………. .

5. Then, Cheng's pare………. came out of the trees.

6. She had been on a hu………. for them.

7. "We are safe! Let's have a fea……….!" said Joe.

Today I scored ☐ out of 7.

Week 8 — Day 5

Look at the picture.
Put a ✔ in the box if the word in bold is spelt correctly and a ✘ if it is not spelt correctly.

He is baking a big cake.

1) **Thay** are in the kitchen.

2) Kai is making cupcakes for **my** birthday.

3) Heidi is helping **mee** bake a cake.

4) **She** stirs the mix in a big bowl.

5) Kai wants to eat **his** cupcakes.

6) **Iy** have mix all over my face!

Today I scored ☐ out of 6.

Week 9 — Day 1

Read each pair of words. Circle the word that is spelt correctly.

1. people / peeple

2. Missis / Mrs

3. put / putt

4. sedd / said

5. cumm / come

6. littel / little

7. asked / asced

8. ies / eyes

Today I scored ☐ out of 8.

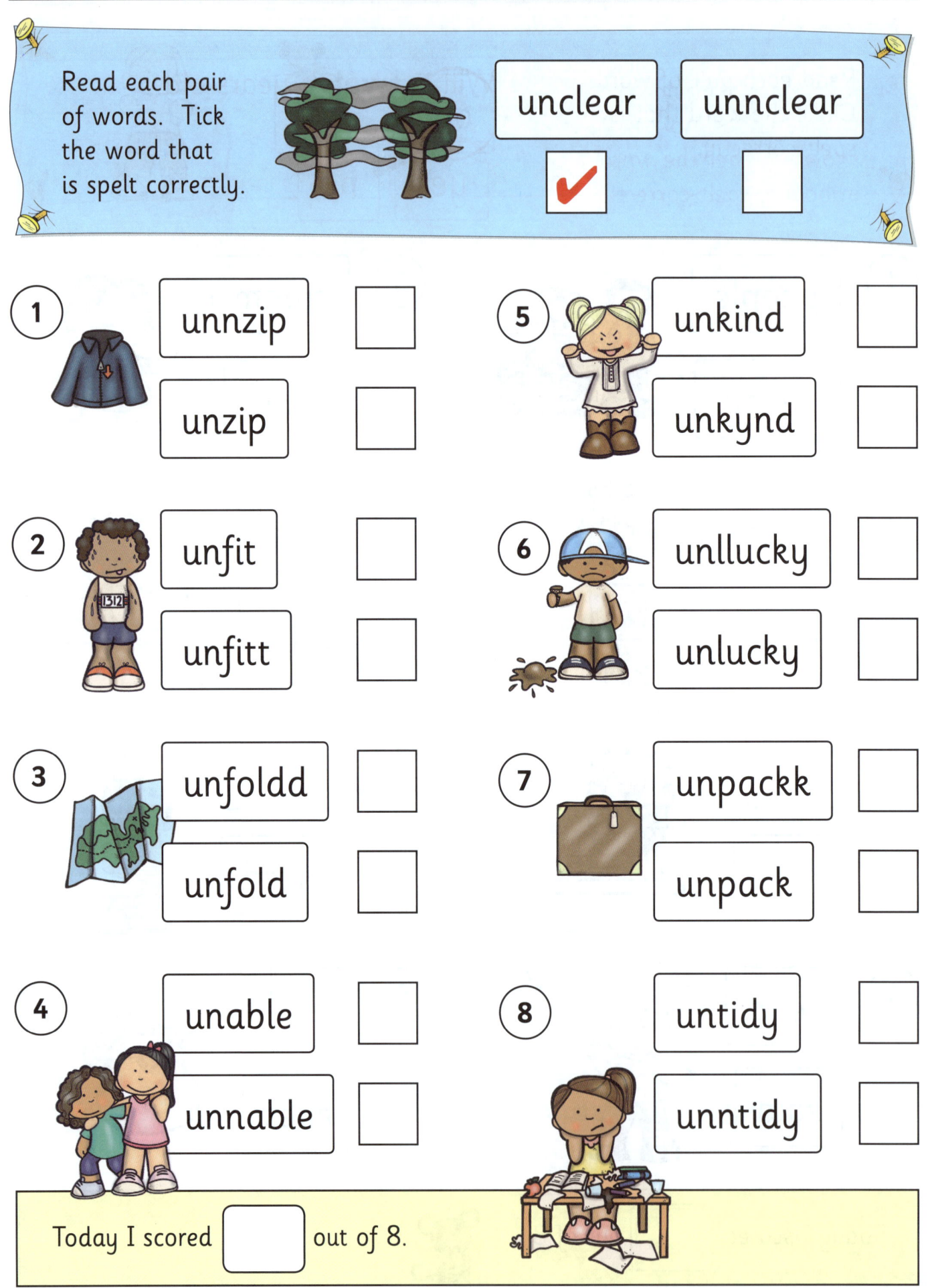

Week 9 — Day 3

Read each sentence. Circle 'yes' or 'no' to show whether the word in bold is spelt correctly.

Will is **twelve** years old.

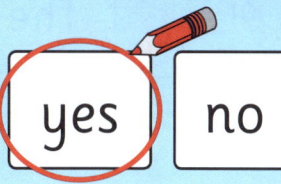 

1) Will **servved** a queen.   yes   no

2) **Thieves** tried to steal from the queen.   yes   no

3) They gave Will a big **shov**.   yes   no

4) Will was very **brayve**.   yes   no

5) He **saved** the queen's gems.   yes   no

6) That was a close **shave**!   yes   no

Today I scored ☐ out of 6.

Week 9 — Day 4

Read each sentence. Fill in the gap with either '**s**' or '**es**' to complete the word.

The bell ring....*s*..... .

1) "Put down your brush..........," says the teacher.

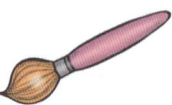

2) Jason rush.......... to finish painting.

3) He want.......... more time.

4) The teacher catch.......... Jason painting.

5) "Other class.......... need the art room!" she says.

6) Jason asks if he can have two more minute.......... .

7) The teacher sigh.......... but nod.......... her head.

Today I scored ☐ out of 8.

Week 9 — Day 5

Look at the picture. Read each sentence. Circle the letters needed to complete the words.

1. Hannah can ___ate.

   st | sk | sp

2. Rex can't ___op!

   sn | sk | st

3. There is lots of ___ow.

   sn | sp | sk

4. Krish is very ___eedy.

   sl | sp | sm

5. The ice is ___ippy!

   st | sn | sl

6. Georgie has a ___edge.

   sm | sl | sk

Today I scored ☐ out of 6.

Week 10 — Day 1

Circle 'yes' or 'no' to show whether each word is spelt correctly.

taler — yes / **no** (circled)

1. oldder — yes / no 
2. harder — yes / no 
3. kindr — yes / no 
4. greattest — yes / no 
5. youngest — yes / no 
6. cleverur — yes / no 
7. softest — yes / no 
8. strongest — yes / no

Today I scored ☐ out of 8.

Week 10 — Day 2

Draw lines to match the words to the correct missing letters. Each word should match the picture shown.

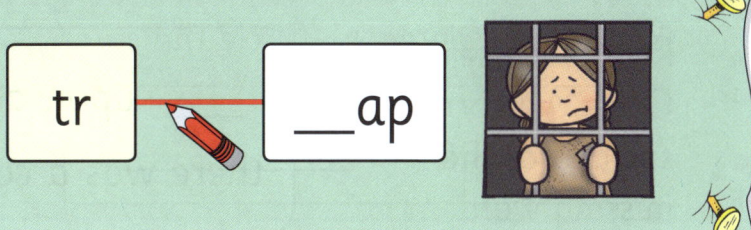

1. 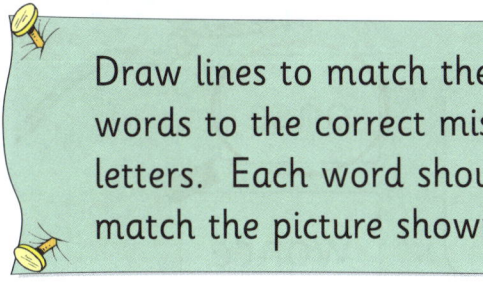 __ime

2.  __eam

3.  __uit

4.  __ophy

cr

dr

tr

fr

5. __ainers

6. __ame

7. ice __eam

8. __awing

Today I scored ☐ out of 8.

Week 10 — Day 3

Read each sentence. Circle the correct spelling of the missing word.

____ upon a time, there was a cowboy.

once (circled)

wonce

1) He was _____ Kevin Cattle.   called   calld

2) Kevin lost some _____ his cows.   ov   of

3) He looked in _____ places.   meny   many

4) _____ could they have gone?   wher   where

5) He _____ the red barn.   checked   cheked

6) "There they are!" Kevin _____.   laughed   laffed

Today I scored ☐ out of 6.

Week 10 — Day 4

Fill in the gap with either 'o' or 'ou' to complete each word.

t…o…day

1) g………

5) l………ve

2) m………se

6) h………se

3) ………ne

7) w………rk

4) m………ntain

8) y………

Today I scored ☐ out of 8.

Week 10 — Day 5

Colour the picture next to each word that is spelt correctly.

Week 11 — Day 1

Read each pair of words. Tick the word that is spelt correctly.

glove ✓ | gluv ☐

1. gaive ☐ | gave ☐
2. have ☐ | hafe ☐
3. save ☐ | sayve ☐
4. olivs ☐ | olives ☐
5. drive ☐ | drivve ☐
6. move ☐ | movv ☐

Today I scored ☐ out of 6.

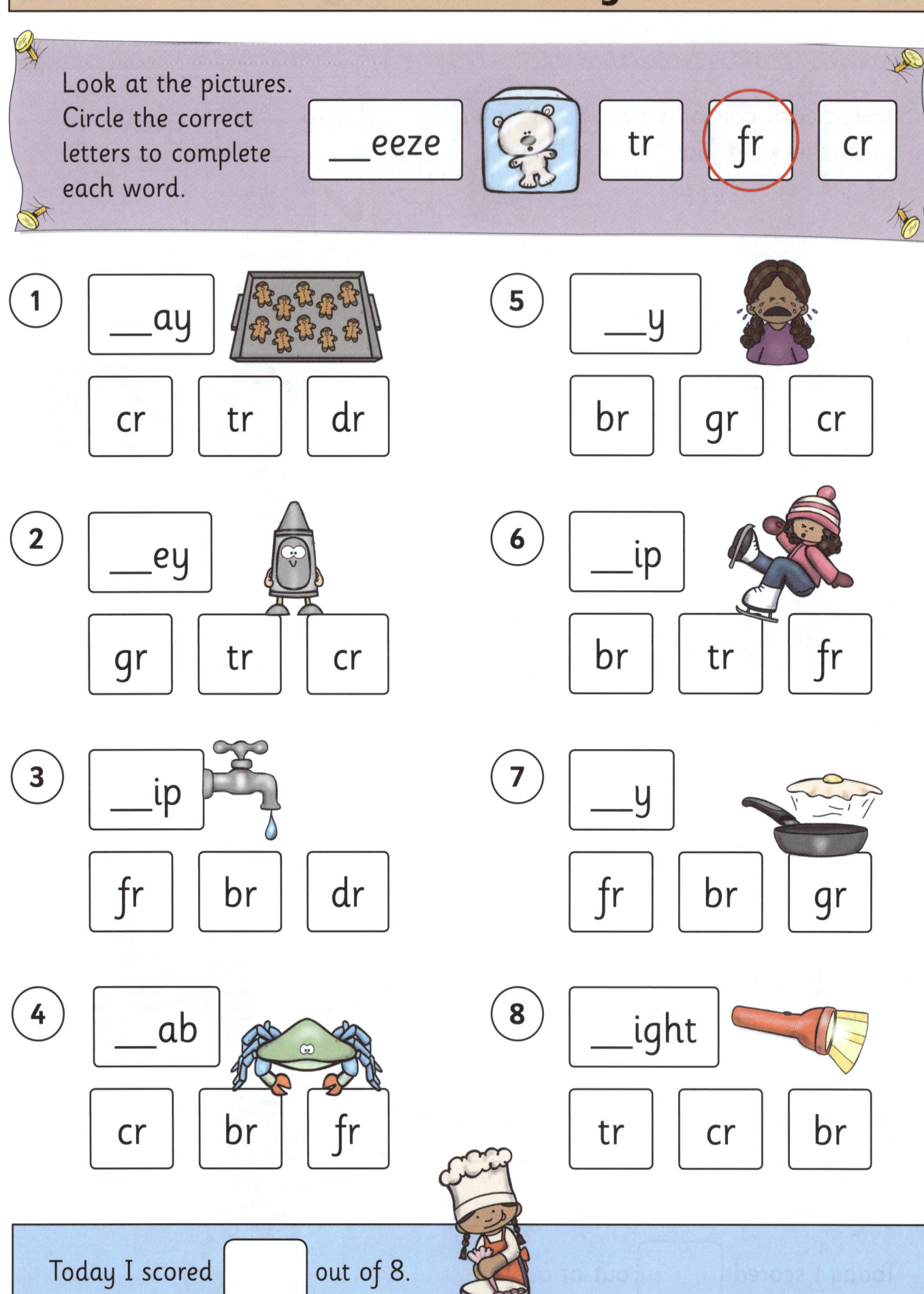

Week 11 — Day 3

Read each pair of sentences. Tick the sentence that is spelt correctly.

An alien was flying. ✓
An alien was flyying. ☐

1) Farmerr Ted saw the ship. ☐
   Farmer Ted saw the ship. ☐

2) The alien landed in a field. ☐
   The alien lannded in a field. ☐

3) The cows started mooing. ☐
   The cows started moing. ☐

4) Ted was very shockeed. ☐
   Ted was very shocked. ☐

5) "Where is your leadr?" said the alien. ☐
   "Where is your leader?" said the alien. ☐

6) "I am tryng to find her." ☐
   "I am trying to find her." ☐

Today I scored ☐ out of 6.

Week 11 — Day 4

Fill in the gap with 'ch', 'sh' or 'th' to complete each word.

 ba.**th**..

1) ………umb

2) ………at

3) slo………

4) ………ell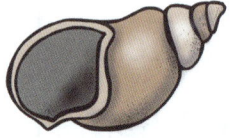

5) wa………

6) ben………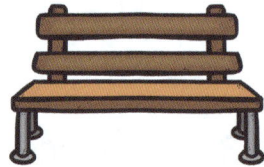

7) ………apes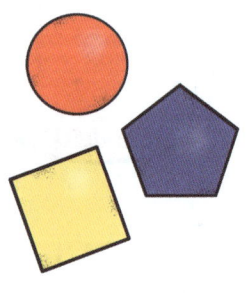

8) ………op

Today I scored ☐ out of 8.

Week 11 — Day 5

Read each sentence. Write the correct spelling of the word in bold.

We are going on **holidai**. ....holiday..........

① I hope it is not **rainee**.

....

② The **lolli** is melting!

....

③ It is **realle** hot here.

....

④ The ice cream is **yumy**.

....

⑤ The beach is **sandee**.

....

Today I scored ☐ out of 5.

Week 12 — Day 1

Circle the word that is spelt correctly in each pair. Draw a line to match each correct word to the picture below.

1. leevs / leaves
2. cayve / cave
3. dove / duv

4. highve / hive
5. dieve / dive
6. wave / wayve

Today I scored ☐ out of 6.

Week 12 — Day 2

Read each sentence. Circle the word in bold if it is spelt correctly. <u>Underline</u> it if it is **not** spelt correctly.

(Mr) Bark lives next door.

He has <u>**sum**</u> pet dogs.

1. **Won** day, he asked me to walk his dogs.

2. "Please don't lose them," he **said**.

3. I told him we would go to **the** park.

4. When we got **ther**, I threw them a ball.

5. Then, lots of different dogs ran to **mee**.

6. They wanted to make **frends**.

7. It **looked** like I had one hundred dogs!

Today I scored ☐ out of 7.

Week 12 — Day 3

Read each sentence. Circle the correct spelling of the word in the box.

He is | uncclean | **(unclean)** .

1) I | unndo | undo | my shirt.

2) The path is | uneeven | uneven .

3) The answer is | uncclear | unclear .

4) The test is | infair | unfair .

5) Amir won't come | unlless | unless | there is cake.

6) She | unncovered | uncovered | the crime.

Today I scored ☐ out of 6.

Week 12 — Day 4

Complete each word so that it matches the picture shown. Fill in the gaps using letters from the boxes.

mi...ss...ion

| ss | zz | ll | ff | ck |

1) spe..........

2)  du..........

3) sni..........

4)  actre..........

5) pi..........a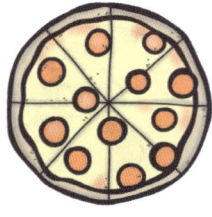

6)  bri..........

7) bu..........y

8)  to..........ee

Today I scored [ ] out of 8.

Week 12 — Day 5

Read the sentences. Rewrite the words in bold adding either 's' or 'es'.

Celia [**dig**] ......digs...... .

1. Laila has found some [**item**] ....

2. Tim [**do**] .... not know what they are.

3. What is that behind the [**bush**] .... ?

4. I think they are old [**bone**] .... !

5. Raj [**like**] .... looking at them.

6. Bjorn [**want**] .... to find some more.

Today I scored ☐ out of 6.

Answers

Week 1 — Day 1
1. padlock
2. digging
3. snowy
4. goalpost
5. apple
6. rabbit

Week 1 — Day 2
1. A crab lives in that **shell**.
2. Watch out for the **bull**!
3. Jim saw me **spill** a drink.
4. Freja was feeling **ill**.
5. Please do not **yell**.
6. The man sat in a **cell**.
7. He nearly **fell** over.

Week 1 — Day 3
1. match
2. watch
3. pitch
4. hutch
5. scratch
6. sketch

Week 1 — Day 4
1. **pl**um
2. **bl**ow
3. **pl**ate
4. **bl**ink
5. **bl**ender
6. **pl**anet

Week 1 — Day 5
1. Colin <u>wos</u> ready to win **some** prizes.
2. **He** had trained <u>al</u> week.
3. Lots of people <u>wer</u> **there** to watch.
4. "Do **you** <u>hav</u> your spear?" the king asked.
5. "<u>Yess</u>, I am ready!" **said** Colin.
6. **Me** and <u>mi</u> friends saw Colin hit <u>tho targot</u>.
7. **We** cheered and roared <u>lyke</u> dragons.

Week 2 — Day 1
1. sent
2. list
3. post
4. vest
5. bent
6. burnt

Week 2 — Day 2
1. he
2. do
3. come
4. what
5. when
6. little

Week 2 — Day 3
1. yes
2. yes
3. no
4. no
5. no
6. yes
7. no
8. no

Week 2 — Day 4
1. The **elf** danced happily.
2. The wizard lost his **belt**.
3. The witch put the frog on a **shelf**.
4. I am wearing a **kilt**.
5. Jack climbed the **tall** vine.
6. She went to **sulk**.

Week 2 — Day 5
1. **sp**lat
2. **sw**eep
3. **sm**ile
4. **sm**ooth
5. **sl**ime
6. **sw**eat
7. **sp**ade
8. **sn**ooze

Week 3 — Day 1
1. **br**ead
2. **cr**ush
3. **cr**ane
4. **dr**ill
5. **dr**um
6. **br**oom
7. **cr**op
8. **dr**ive

Week 3 — Day 2
1. highest
2. coldest
3. shortest
4. quickest
5. strongest
6. slowest

Week 3 — Day 3
1.
2.
3.
4.
5.
6.

Week 3 — Day 4
1. Yaro enjoys **going** up mountains.
2. Shannon is **resting** on the sofa.
3. The plane is **landing** on the runway.
4. Annie is **asking** a question.
5. I like **watching** films at the cinema.
6. The horse is **leaping** over the fence.

Week 3 Day 5
1. Mia sees something huge and **gr**een.
2. "Oh no, it's a **tr**oll!" she cries.
3. Jack shakes and **gr**oans quietly.
4. "It's okay, I'm **fr**iendly," says the troll.
5. Behind Mia, Jack is **fr**ozen in fear.
6. "What if it's a **tr**ick?" he asks.
7. Mia **gr**ins and goes to say hello.

Week 4 — Day 1
1. ✔   6. ✘
2. ✘   7. ✔
3. ✘   8. ✔
4. ✘   9. ✘
5. ✔   10. ✔

Week 4 — Day 2
1. so**ld**   5. me**lt**
2. ho**ld**   6. fe**lt**
3. gu**lp**   7. bo**lt**
4. co**ld**   8. he**lp**

Week 4 — Day 3
1. My jumper is **itchy**.
2. My **teacher** is friendly.
3. Arham left his shoes in the **porch**.
4. Dad made a **batch** of cookies.
5. We go to the zoo on a **coach**.
6. I have a pair of **crutches**.

Week 4 — Day 4
1. Everyone is at Jane's (**party**).
2. We watch the **funnee** clown.
3. The cake was not (**easy**) to make.
4. It is a nice, (**sunny**) day.
5. Jane's **familee** are here.
6. She is (**very**) glad they came.
7. Jane is **happi** with her presents.

Week 4 — Day 5
1. ho**nk**   4. tru**nk**
2. pi**nk**   5. sku**nk**
3. su**nk**   6. dri**nk**

Week 5 — Day 1
1. softer   4. warmer
2. quicker 5. louder
3. slower   6. lighter

Week 5 — Day 2
1. so**ck**
2. ki**ck**
3. ba**ck**
4. par**k**
5. li**ck**
6. shru**nk**

Week 5 — Day 3
1. Be careful not to **slip**!
2. She has a **black** cat.
3. Miles has **blond** hair.
4. The pig **plods** in the mud.
5. My pencil is **blunt**.
6. He raced down the **slope**.

Week 5 — Day 4
1. **ch**ips   5. pa**th**
2. **ch**ain   6. **sh**ip
3. **sh**ort   7. **ch**in
4. pin**ch**   8. **th**orn

Week 5 — Day 5
1. Yulia is **glad** she won.
2. The moon **glows** in the sky.
3. We make **clay** pots.
4. The **clock** ticks loudly.
5. I can **click** my fingers.
6. Jimmy looks at the **globe**.

Week 6 — Day 1
1. fast   5. pant
2. ant   6. point
3. post   7. toast
4. grunt   8. lost

Week 6 — Day 2
1. hi**ll**
2. loa**f**
3. we**ll**
4. ow**l**
5. cli**ff**
6. do**ll**

Week 6 — Day 3
1. splashes
2. sprays
3. runs
4. catches
5. drips
6. smiles

Week 6 — Day 4
1. The party **is** today.
2. There will **be** cake.
3. Bring **your** wand.
4. **No** dragons can come.
5. Can you come **to** the party?

Week 6 — Day 5
1. no
2. yes
3. yes
4. no
5. no
6. yes

Week 7 — Day 1
1. reading
2. brushed
3. boxer
4. eating
5. singer
6. cheering
7. splashed
8. baker

Week 7 — Day 2
1. yes
2. no
3. yes
4. yes
5. no
6. no

Week 7 — Day 3
1. **c**law
2. **s**lug
3. **c**limb
4. **s**low
5. **s**lide
6. **c**lub
7. **s**lip
8. **c**logs

Week 7 — Day 4
1. gold
2. calf
3. milk
4. salt
5. yelp
6. adult

Week 7 — Day 5
1. Rob feels **unsafe**.
2. Jack and Tina **unload** the car.
3. Kim **unties** Atalia's shoelace.
4. Grace **unlocks** the door.
5. Imani is **unhappy**.
6. Barney is **unwell**.

Week 8 — Day 1
1. ki**ng**
2. wi**nk**
3. lo**ng**
4. ba**ng**
5. si**nk**
6. thi**nk**
7. wi**ng**
8. tha**nk**

Week 8 — Day 2
1. friend
2. school
3. love
4. full
5. push
6. pull

Week 8 — Day 3
1. Adam lifts the **heavy** weight.
2. Helen is trying **archery**.
3. We **enjoy** rowing.
4. I was **angry** when I lost.
5. Fred is running the **relay** race.
6. The winner's medal is really **shiny**.
7. We **play** hockey every day.

Week 8 — Day 4
1. They had been walking in the fore**st** for hours.
2. "I wa**nt** to go home!" said Joe.
3. "Let's sit down and re**st**," sighed Cheng.
4. They sat down by a big pla**nt**.
5. Then, Cheng's pare**nt** came out of the trees.
6. She had been on a hu**nt** for them.
7. "We are safe! Let's have a fea**st**!" said Joe.

Week 8 — Day 5
1. ✗
2. ✓
3. ✗
4. ✓
5. ✓
6. ✗

Week 9 — Day 1
1. people
2. Mrs
3. put
4. said
5. come
6. little
7. asked
8. eyes

Week 9 — Day 2
1. unzip
2. unfit
3. unfold
4. unable
5. unkind
6. unlucky
7. unpack
8. untidy

Week 9 — Day 3
1. no
2. yes
3. no
4. no
5. yes
6. yes

Week 9 — Day 4
1. "Put down your brush**es**," says the teacher.
2. Jason rush**es** to finish painting.
3. He want**s** more time.
4. The teacher catch**es** Jason painting.
5. "Other class**es** need the art room!" she says.
6. Jason asks if he can have two more minute**s**.
7. The teacher sigh**s**, but nod**s** her head.

Week 9 — Day 5
1. **sk**ate
2. **st**op
3. **sn**ow
4. **sp**eedy
5. **sl**ippy
6. **sl**edge

Week 10 — Day 1

1. no
2. yes
3. no
4. no
5. yes
6. no
7. yes
8. yes

Week 10 — Day 2

1. **cr**ime
2. **dr**eam
3. **fr**uit
4. **tr**ophy
5. **tr**ainers
6. **fr**ame
7. ice **cr**eam
8. **dr**awing

Week 10 — Day 3

1. He was **called** Kevin Cattle.
2. Kevin lost some **of** his cows.
3. He looked in **many** places.
4. **Where** could they have gone?
5. He **checked** the red barn.
6. "There they are!" Kevin **laughed**.

Week 10 — Day 4

1. g**o**
2. m**ou**se
3. **o**ne
4. m**ou**ntain
5. l**o**ve
6. h**ou**se
7. w**o**rk
8. y**ou**

Week 10 — Day 5

Week 11 — Day 1

1. gave
2. have
3. save
4. olives
5. drive
6. move

Week 11 — Day 2

1. **tr**ay
2. **gr**ey
3. **dr**ip
4. **cr**ab
5. **cr**y
6. **tr**ip
7. **fr**y
8. **br**ight

Week 11 — Day 3

1. **Farmer** Ted saw the ship.
2. The alien **landed** in a field.
3. The cows started **mooing**.
4. Ted was very **shocked**.
5. "Where is your **leader**?" said the alien.
6. "I am **trying** to find her."

Week 11 — Day 4

1. **th**umb
2. **ch**at
3. **sl**oth
4. **sh**ell
5. wa**sh**
6. ben**ch**
7. **sh**apes
8. **sh**op

Week 11 — Day 5

1. I hope it is not **rainy**.
2. The **lolly** is melting!
3. It is **really** hot here.
4. The ice cream is **yummy**.
5. The beach is **sandy**.

Week 12 — Day 1

1. leaves
2. cave
3. dove
4. hive
5. dive
6. wave

Week 12 — Day 2

1. **Won** day, he asked me to walk his dogs.
2. "Please don't lose them," he (said).
3. I told him we would go to (the) park.
4. When we got **ther**, I threw them a ball.
5. Then, lots of different dogs ran to **mee**.
6. They wanted to make **frends**.
7. It (looked) like I had one hundred dogs!

Week 12 — Day 3

1. I **undo** my shirt.
2. The path is **uneven**.
3. The answer is **unclear**.
4. The test is **unfair**.
5. Amir won't come **unless** there is cake.
6. She **uncovered** the crime.

Week 12 — Day 4

1. spe**ll**
2. du**ck**
3. sni**ff**
4. actre**ss**
5. pi**zz**a
6. bri**ck**
7. bu**ll**y
8. to**ff**ee

Week 12 — Day 5

1. Laila has found some item**s**.
2. Tim do**es** not know what they are.
3. What is that behind the bush**es**?
4. I think they are old bon**es**!
5. Raj like**s** looking at them.
6. Bjorn want**s** to find some more.